AMEN
THE PRINCIPLE OF PEACE

Story by: Yogi Ebony Smith

Published by Melanin Origins
PO Box 122123; Arlington, TX 76012
All rights reserved, including the right of reproduction in whole
or in part in any form.
Copyright 2022

Second Edition

The author asserts the moral right under the Copyright, Designs and Patents Act of 1988 to be identified as the author of this work.

This novel is a work of fiction. The names, characters and incidents portrayed in the work, other than those clearly in the public domain, are of the author's imagination and are not to be construed as real. Any resemblance to actual persons, living or dead, events or localities, is entirely coincidental.

All rights reserved. No part of this publication may be reproduced, stored in a retrieval system or transmitted, in any form by any means without the prior consent of the author, nor be otherwise circulated in any form of binding or cover other than that with which it is published and without a similar condition being imposed on the subsequent purchaser.

Series Editors: Reginald Robinson; Lenny Williams, & Shiree Fowler

Library of Congress Control Number: 2021946257

ISBN: 978-1-62676-444-6 hardback

ISBN: 978-1-62676-443-9 paperback

ISBN: 978-1-62676-458-3 ebook

THE PRINCIPLE OF AMEN

There is peace in the depths of the ocean. A calm and a stillness that is totally unmoved by chaos occurring on the surface top. That is the peace that you are.

Remain graceful as you express your truth in love.

www.MelaninOrigins.com

PEACE is harmony that comes from deep within;

A joy that flows from the inside out.

PEACE teaches us to love and make new friends;

A heart filled with **PEACE** has no room for doubt.

Let's see what girls and boys around the world do everyday

To create **PEACE** and happiness in their very own way.

My name is JAYA and I live in India. Shanti is how we say PEACE.

I create shanti everyday

by taking deep breaths in and out, my way!

One hand on my belly;
One hand on my heart.
Deep breaths in and out
That's how my PEACE comes about.

My name is **MAYA** and I'm from Mexico.

Paz is how we say **PEACE**.

I create paz everyday
by spending time in nature.
Hugging a tree or smelling flowers
can bring me PEACE for hours and hours.

With my knees on the mat and both hands by my chest,

I am reminded of the importance of each and every breath.

My name is LUCA and I live in Italy.
PACE is how we say PEACE.
I find pace everyday
by relaxing in my own way.

Feet up with a good book in hand;

PEACE takes me to a joyful land.

Where worry and doubt have no place to stay;

A place where happiness always comes my way.

I create **PEACE** everyday by dancing my worries away.

I dance to my own rhythm;

I dance to my own beat.

Every step I take brings me more **PEACE**.

My name is Malia and I live in Hawaii.
Malu is how we say PEACE.

I practice yoga everyday
to create PEACE my way.
Forward folds and down dogs
Help me find PEACE through it all.

My name is **AUSET** and I live in Egypt.

HETEP is how we say **PEACE**.

I pray for world **PEACE** before I go to bed,

And when I say amen, I feel **PEACE** come over me.

I put my head on pillow and snuggle up tight;

This peaceful feeling helps me rest with ease all night.

It's important to find **PEACE** in everything you do;

I AM **PEACE** and so are you.

PEACE during the day and **PEACE** at night.

How do you bring **PEACE** into your life?

Modern Day Melanin Origins

Insert Name:

You are the change the world has been searching for. You have everything you need, within you, to create peaceful and beautiful realities for yourself and those you love most. The Ancient Egyptians believed the Tree of Life existed in every human being and MA'AT was the spiritual and cultural system that helped Nile Valley citizens realize their divine nature. The very first realization that must be made is that

YOU are peace.

If you create from a place of peace... you'd be well on your way to being one of the next Modern Day Melanin Origins.
Amen.

www.ingramcontent.com/pod-product-compliance
Lightning Source LLC
Chambersburg PA
CBHW040006080526
44586CB00027B/2894